MW01519936

FOR THE LOVE OF CORVETTES - TABLE OF CONTENTS

All rights reserved
Copyright Applied for, 2/6/2018 by Dale Snipes
Cover Copyright Applied for, 2/6/2018 by Dale Snipes

Available from Amazon.com
and other retail outlets

FOR THE LOVE OF CORVETTES

CORVETTE STORIES

JERRY AND DALE - Sandpoint, ID

Jerry, a retired policeman who later worked for FEMA and traveled to disasters all over the world, had been a "first responder" at the 911 tragedy.   While there working as the head of security for all the entities that were helping over 600 people a day he lost 70+% of his lungs to the bad air.   He has been on oxygen ever since.   Jerry and Dale both rode motorcycles for years, but it became increasing hard for Jerry as he could not use his oxygen on the bike. So, he finally had to sell his bike.   HOWEVER nothing was going to keep this good man down.   They decided they could have just as much fun with a Corvette.

They had been looking for a certain model for some time with no luck.   It was time for Jerry's yearly "man trip" hunting with his sons, so off he went. Dale told him that as sure as he got up in the mountains, out of phone contact, she was bound to find just the right car.   He said he would come to the top of the mountain every night and call her, just in case she did find something.

He left at 4:00 am the next morning.   And, would you believe, when the paper came out that morning, sure enough there was a photo of the car they were looking for.   Now Dale was not completely up on all the bells and whistles that Corvettes came with, but she told the dealer what Jerry wanted and he said that was exactly what that car had.   It was on sale for considerable less than the prices they had been getting, so she went from their place in Sandpoint, Idaho to the dealer in Spokane, Washington, over 100 miles away, to see it. There it was, TA DA!!! It was beautiful. So she called Jerry, actually about six times to get his ok. They planned on each of them paying half the cost but she wanted to make sure he was good with it. It took several hours before he came to the top of the mountain and got the messages. He kept asking, "Is it a Grand Sport?" The dealer said that is was, and Dale didn't know the difference. She asked if they could hold it two more days until Jerry got back, but they said that when they have something listed in the paper "on sale" for that much off , it is illegal to hold it without a deposit, if someone comes to buy it.

Dale was unable to get Jerry on the phone again so she decided to go for it. She paid 1/2 down and took the car home. The dealer actually drove it to their house and had a salesman follow to give him a ride back as Dale had to drive her car back.

When Jerry got home, here was this beautiful car in the garage. But, guess what? It was NOT a Grand Sport. It was however everything else they had been looking for and Jerry, although disappointed was reasonably gallant about the whole thing.

They had several great trips in that car. They did a tour of all the west coast National Parks, and visited friends in six different states. Got a lot of "OOOHH", and "AHHHHH". on the way.

Later that summer, Jerry went on a "Man Trip", with his best friend Paul. They drove the Corvette to Austin, Texas to see the Corvette racing team compete in the American Le Mans race at the Circuit of the Americas. Jerry said they had a wonderful time and he won the award for driving the furthers.

After the races, Corvette held an awards dinner for everyone who won an award. The "Corvette Girls", were there as well as the host. These beautiful young ladies were able to pay their college expenses with the money they made working for the Corvette tours and events. Jerry was VERY impressed with how intelligent and witty they were.

Jerry has always been good at "one liners", and had everyone laughing. Then, one of the "Corvette Girls" came up to him and rubbed him on the head and said, "You are so cute, I would like to take you home with me." "Jerry said, "You know what, unless you need a pillow, I wouldn't be any good to you!!" Everyone just roared!!!

When the new 2015 LS2 Corvette Stingray came out they decided they HAD to have it. They placed their order and waited. They planed to trade in their 2012 and the dealer told them if they would do so then, even though they would not be getting the new car for another month, he would give them an extra $3,000 for it as they could sell it right away. If they waited until the new car came, they would be well into the "off season" and sports cars do not move well in the winter. They agreed, but the delivery of their car was put off twice due to a recall and a "longshoreman" strike.

Well the dealer bought it and since it was both clean and low mileage they displayed it right in front of their lot. On the second night there, a drunk driver came speeding around the corner and hit that car and four Camaros. OHHHHHHHH!!

They finally got the new car and would you believe, it snowed going over the pass on the way home. Their beautiful new car spent the next few months in the garage.

One of the perks the company offered was a $2,000.00 off on the opportunity to attend the Ron Fellows driving school in Pahrump, Nevada. It seems that there were so many new things to learn about their car that Chevrolet found that most of the new owners were having trouble learning it all. They decided to go and it was probably the best decision they ever made. "Pahrump is Indian for water that comes out of the rock".

The school was two days, the condo was wonderfully equipped, the food was great and the instructors were incredible. They were very good and knowledgeable in every aspect. Jerry and Dale learned more about their car in that short time then they could possibly have learned on their own. They got to drive the school's Corvettes on the track, learned all the various modes to travel in, drove on all different surfaces, and learned new ways to start quickly without "burning rubber". (Dale got in trouble for doing that though). she drove a drag race car in the old days when she was a LOT younger and "trophyed", seven out of seven. She learned to get off just as quickly at the school, without "burning rubber".

They had them start out fast, suddenly break and spin the wheel and of course they spun out. Then they wet the track and even added silicone, had them put their cars in "wet weather" mode and do the same thing. THEY COULD NOT SPIN OUT!!! It was pretty amazing.
At the end of the course they each got to do "hot" laps riding with a pro, around the track. They thought THEY were doing "fast laps", until they rode with them. WOW!!!

It was great fun and they met a lot of great people as well.

<u>Jerry on the track at driving school</u> ------------------------------ <u>Dale on the same track</u>

Jerry and Dale would like to recommend this class to anyone who gets the chance to take it. Don't miss this opportunity if at all possible.

One of their favorite trips is to Monetary Calif. to the Mazda Raceway. There is an event there every year that they really enjoy. One of the high lights is the annual "Corrals" for various models of cars. They always enjoy parking in the "Corvette Corral". There are well over 200 Corvettes parked there from all over the country. What a beautiful sight. And, this is only one of 4 rows of Corvettes.

There are "Corrals" for Ford GTs", Mazda's, Porsche etc. but the Corvette Corral always has more cars than all of the others put together.

During the three day event they stayed in a V.I.P. suite. They had front row balcony seats over-looking the race track and the pit area. They were served two meals per day and all the drinks they wanted. This included soda, coffee, tea, beer and wine.

They also enjoyed walking or in some cases flagging down a ride with the folks that provided free service around the grounds. There were innumerable booths selling souvenirs, clothing, car products and all sorts of food and treat items.

The most exciting part of the trip was the ability to visit the pit area, where Dale was privileged to meet Dan Binks, crew chief for the #3 car of the Corvette racing team.   He was gracious enough to
let her take a photo of the two of them standing in front of the famous #3 Corvette race car.

They also got to meet the racing team drivers and got a wonderful autographed photo from them.

We are all so proud of these excellent drivers and mechanics that keep these awesome Corvettes winning. Even though the racing "Balance of Performance" puts so many restrictions on them. They keep making Corvette add weight and reduce restrictor size. BUT they still keep winning!

*Author's note, "Why do they not instruct the other manufactures to improve THEIR cars instead? After all the Corvette engine is a standard push-rod engine, reasonably low tech but very reliable. On the other hand, other manufacturers have developed high tech, high revolution, smaller displacement turbo engines that are more complicated and a LOT more expensive.

It seems that all rules do not apply to all manufactures. For instance the two classes that race together are the GTLM (production cars available to the general public, usually running under $100,000.00) and the PROTO TYPE RACING CARS. All the manufactures, with the exception of the Ford GT abide by this rule. The Ford GT is way out of the range of the general public at $250,000.00 and should be running in the Proto type class, but is running instead in the GTLM class.

In spite of this, the Corvette team finished 3rd and 4th in this years (2018) Rolex 24 hour, Daytona, Florida race. Congratulations folks. You are one awesome team.

Jerry and Dale also got to drive their car around the race track. They had to sign a release and agreed not to go over 50 miles per hour. There were about 50 other Corvettes, and we all MAY have gone a LITTLE faster.

When they got to Monetary, they wanted to get the car washed before they went to the raceway. It was really dirty after traveling all the way from Sandpoint, Idaho.

However it was **"AGAINST THE LAW",** to hand wash a car, because of the water shortage in California.!

After leaving Monetary, they decided to drive up the coast on Hwy. 1 to the Redwoods. It was a beautiful drive with the ocean below and the mountains and forests all around. But, it was a very long drive with far too much construction. When they arrived at the south end of the giant red woods, the tree they were hoping to photograph with the car going through, it was "CLOSED". Further north however there were two other "drive through" trees, so they headed on. Since then that tree went down in a bad storm. What a shame to such a beautiful gift of nature. When they finally got there, guess what? The Corvette was too wide to fit through the tree. . So they took the following photos of the car parked just outside the tree from the front and back.

When they owned the 2012 Corvette they got together with a great group of folks from the North Idaho area and formed the North Idaho Corvette Club. There are 22 members now . They also travel with the Spokane, Wa. Corvette Club. These are an awesome bunch people and we hope you will enjoy their stories and photo of their cars that will appear in the following pages.

_____

CHUCK AND LORIE ADAMS - Coeur d' Alene, ID

We bought our 1994 ZR1 in November of 1998. The following May we went on a trip to the awesome Big Sky Corvette Meet, Porker Run and car show in Montana.   This is a yearly event that starts at a different location in Montana each time.   It is put on by different Montana Corvette clubs each year. There is always a big turn out and is a well planned and well run event. Check out the Montana web site for details about the next show coming up in May.

This is on the memorial day weekend.   After the first day we were heading back to our motel and heard that rain was in the forecast.   Sure enough the rain started and we started to put our windows up.   The window on the passenger side would NOT go up.   We tried everything.   When we got to our motel Chuck worked on it for some time, to no avail.   It was getting chilly as the rain continued and I was really getting cold.   We were getting a little desperate.   We did not want to get the car wet inside, not to mention us as well.

 After trying everything we could, we finally gave up and got a plastic bag and some duck tape and used this for a "Mickey mouse" repair job.   It was pretty embarrassing, here we were in this beautiful Corvette with the window covered with a trash bag and duck tape. AHHHHHHHHHHHH!!!!

We ended up having to travel all the way home to Coeur d' Alene with our trash bag and duck taped window. I was freezing the whole way. Even days later, we were unable to get it fixed.   Every time we went anywhere I was cold. The window was still down and the air was still cold out.

Then one after noon, Chuck got extremely frustrated and shut the door, harder than usual. THE WINDOW WENT UP!!!!! - -   After that it worked well, and has ever since.   That was 18 years ago and it is still working.   It has never happened again.   Was this a mysterious Gremlin???

Chuck is now the President of the North Idaho Corvette club and doing an awesome job.

We really didn't want to trade in the green car but when we were at the dealer and saw this beauty, we fell in love. We HAD to have it!   Not only was it a beautiful RED color, but had more of everything including MORE ROOM.   So, we drove home in our brand new car.

The first thing we did was to drive it over to our friends house. They really like it. Then we went to the next meeting of the North Idaho Corvette Club everyone there was wondering who the heck was in that awesome red Vet???

We have really enjoyed the car and already won a few awards showing it at meets. At the Big Sky, Montana meet we won a nice 3rd place trophy for C6 Show and Shine, then at the Wallace, Idaho, "32 Year, Wallace Depot Days," we won a trophy for "Outstanding Entry".

THE ATOMIC ORANGE SAGA
BILL AND LEE ANN MOORE - Dalton Gardens, ID

I had been a typical red blooded American boy in 1966 and "lusted" after a Corvette ever since then. AND as everyone knows who has ever owned one, once you have one you will never be happy with out one." I suppose I should start at the beginning and tell you about my first Vet.

#1 - I had a "near death" experience about 20 years ago when my appendix burst. It made me think, it was time to go for my dream. So my wife and I started looking around on "eBay" in the Corvette section and found one we liked. It was in Los Angles, Calif. and we were in North Idaho. I called the seller, who was a dealer there, and talked to him on the phone for 3 hours! I was impressed with what he had to say, so I hired an appraisal company to test drive it and to appraise it's over-all condition. They sent back a glowing report, and the dealer sent 30+ photos, showing every bit of the car, inside and out. So, we got serious. Near the end of the bidding on eBay, I was competing with one other person and kept going back and forth as we both tried to out-bid the other.

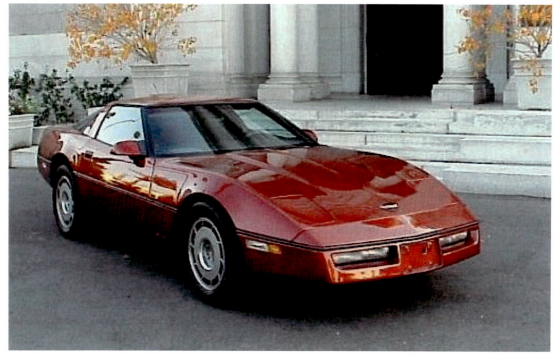

The wife and I had decided in advance that we would not go over $10,000. We had planned to add a big new deck to our house, and wanted to be sure we could still do so after buying a new car.   At the last minute, as I watched the clock running down, she was hovering over me. I said, "You know, if we get the Vette, we won't be able to build the new deck." She put her chin on my shoulder and whispered into my ear, "Bill, this is the Bad Angle, forget the deck, get the Vette." Then she put her chin on my other shoulder and whispered, "This is the Good Angle, forget the deck, get the Vette." I pushed the button at the last second for my final bid, and WON!

Even though they had to ship it from California it was still under $10,000. However, since it was winter here, it had to stay in the garage until spring. The wait was killing me! When Spring arrived I drove that car around town for *days!*

Corvette #2 When it came time for a new one, we went to the largest on-line community in the world of Corvette owners, the Corvette Forum. We found a C5 in Dallas and bought it. It was a 2000 convertible, Navy blue. We flew out to pick it up and took our time, (2 1/2 weeks) coming home, stopping at the Corvette Museum on the way.

Now, #3   A few years later, we decided that a convertible wasn't for us so we decided to look at a newer Vette,   We went on a club event to a car show in Missoula, Montana. This is a yearly event put on by local Montana Corvette clubs and in a different in-state location each year. The "host" hotel just happened to be across the street from the local Chevy dealer. Of course he had his supply of Corvettes right in front.

The Chevy dealer hosted a welcome night and served beer and wine with snacks and encouraged everyone to look at his Corvettes. We went over and walked around the Vettes. Here was a new 2007 "Atomic Orange" C6 coupe. We fell in love with the color and took a test drive. Hooked!

The next morning, I was in back of the hotel washing my car and getting it clean. I was telling a friend about the Atomic Orange Vette and how I would love to have it. However I would need to sell my present car before I could buy it. Right then a guy walked up behind me as I was washing my car and tapped me on my shoulder and said, "I heard what you said about the car, maybe we should talk."

The next day, a deal was made and he drove home to Seattle, and we drove home in our new Atomic Orange Vet, for the world to see! I still have that car, and it's still a real head turner!

RICHARD AND LESLEY TATE - Careywood, ID

September 2014 I got my first Corvette. A brand new 2015 Shark Gray Stingray coupe. I was excited as one can get at age 70.

Found every excuse to take a drive for the first couple of weeks. came home one afternoon in a hurry, pulled into the garage, pushed the ignition off button, jumped out and went into the house. Forgot one small item. The car does not have to be in park to shut if off as there is no key. Left the car in drive, come out the next morning and the battery was dead as the proverbial door knob.

All electronic systems stay on if car is in drive! Doors locked tight, electronic key fob useless. Needless to say, I had not read the owners manual carefully.

Can't get in the car, now what? Called the Chevy dealer and found out about the emergency key in the key fob that opens the back hatch. Opened the hatch but couldn't reach the door latch. Called the Chevy dealer back and found out about the emergency door release cord in the back.

Car is now open, popped the hood and can't find the battery. Third call to the dealer, batters is in back hatch under the mat. After some searching, (not easy to access) found the battery and hooked up to my trusty battery charger. Car started in about an hour and all was well.

Guess the moral of this story is "Learn a little bit about your fancy new Corvette."
          Have enjoyed many fun hours in my Vette since that day!

PEGGY AND TERRY BURNS - Spokane, WA

I have thought about your request for Corvette stories. Don't have anything for the 2014, but the following is one for the 2008 silver Corvette. Our very first one. I attached a picture of it. Not a good picture, but don't really have many.

We purchased our first Corvette in 2008. We live in Washington and we purchased it in Montana. We drove one of our vehicles there and agreed that we would trade off driving the new car home. While I was driving we were somewhere in either Montana or Idaho. We were stopped for road construction. I had the top down. The young lady who was the flagger walked over to me and said "Wow, what a pretty **MUSTANG!!!!!!!!** I laughed and then said "It isn't a Mustang it's a Corvette". She was a little embarrassed. I told Terry the next time we stopped to trade off drivers. He laughed too and now we have a funny story to tell about our first Corvette.

These folks loved their Corvette so much they bought a beautiful blue new 2014.

They went right to the manufacture in Bowling Green, Kentucky. the first two photos are of the beautiful new Corvette in front of the Corvette Museum there.

Here are two pictures of the 2014 Corvette in front of the Corvette Museum in Bowling Green, KY

Back in Spokane, Washington

This summer we were gone for 2 months in the car. Left on 6/1 and returned home 8/1. We traveled 13,834 miles through 30 states plus Washington DC. Weather varied from 115 in Death Valley, CA to

40's in Wyoming. Drove through many deluges of rain, particularly in the south, where everyone, even on the freeway, just pulled over until it eased up enough to see more than 5 feet in front of you.

Many people made comments about how nice the car was. Our favorite was a lady at a hotel somewhere who said "You guys sure have a cute little blue car." Also we had many offers of trades from old beaters to a new Cadillac Escalade. The Escalade was at a hotel where the driver was loading about five passengers and their luggage. We asked him where he planned to put the passengers and luggage if we traded and he said they would be on their own.

No problems with the car, although we had to get the oil changed twice and had to replace the front tires toward the end of the trip. We drove through just about any type of scenery you could imagine from mountains, plains, desert, ocean, rolling hills, farmland, etc. We also averaged 29.8 miles per gallon during the trip, which was fantastic. We had a great time. Good thing it was summer so we didn't need much clothing except shorts and tops because as you know the trunk is TINY, particularly since the top takes up a lot room.

We really enjoy our new car and have continued to go on trips on our own, or with other Corvette owners.

LARRY & JEANITA GRINDER - Coeur d'Alene, ID

Larry and his wife Jeanette got their first Corvette, a white 1985 a few years earlier. They enjoyed several great jaunts around their home area in Coeur d'Alene, Idaho.   They took turns driving and Jeanette probably drove the Corvette more that Larry did.   She really enjoyed it. However she did not like to drive it on the freeways. Then one day, Larry drove it to his accountant's house to deliver some records so that the accountant could work on his taxes.   When the accountant saw the Corvette he told Larry that his father, that recently passed away had twelve Corvettes. They were doled out to relatives and the accountant ended up with four of them. He asked Larry if he would like to see them.   Of course Larry said he would.

One of the Corvettes really caught Larry's eye. It was a '93 Ruby Red 3rd Anniversary coupe. Larry knew that there were a limited number of them built and he really liked it.   The accountant said he would give him a great deal on it if he was interested.   He also said he would be willing to take his white Corvette in as part of the trade.   Larry couldn't resist and made the deal. He had actually been thinking of getting a newer car so it wasn't too hard for the accountant to talk him into it.   The accountant pointed out that because it was a "rare" model folks would be looking at it and it would be a great conversation piece. Not to mention a great investment. It would just increase in value if he took good care of it. On top of that it had just 70,000 miles on it.

One Sunday Larry decided to drive the Corvette to church. His wife Jeanette did not go that day. One of the women members came to him, after church and said that it had always been on her "Bucket List" to ride in a Corvette.   Larry knew she was a nice person so he decided to give her a ride.   Larry lived near Hayden lake in Northern Idaho. The lake has several miles of shore line with all kinds of twists and turns.   The speed limit signs at the turns usually advise, "15 miles per hr." Of course in a Corvette you HAVE to go a little faster.   I think it is some kind of rule, isn't it?
Well, she was holding on tight, but having a lot of fun.   When they got back she thanked Larry for a great time and for satisfying a part of her bucket list wish.

DAVE & MARIA FELLOWS - Hayden, ID

Dave had been a Corvette addict since he was 16 yrs. old. Even then, he wanted one so badly that he got a job and bought one himself. That was quite an accomplishment for a sixteen year old. BUT, he persisted and finally got one. Over the years he had several others as well. Maria had a Viper, but they both decided that they really, really wanted the new Corvette.

One very rainy day they heard about a Corvette that was available at a dealer in Spokane, Washington. When they got there, they saw a beautiful midnight blue 2014 model and fell in love with it. They really liked it but decided to go home and think it over. Well that didn't take long. They went back and bought it. After they picked it up, they went to dinner then the very next day drove it to their children's homes to show it off. All the grand kids wanted a ride and Dave took each one on a short drive. They all loved the car and made quite a fuss over it.

Shortly there after they became involved in the Spokane Corvette club and the club took a trip to St. Johns, Washington. It seems there was a parade there that day and when the city heard that 35 Corvettes were coming, decided to hold the parade up until they got there and had them lead the parade. What fun!

Later they went to visit the local dam. Normally the folks there, only allowed one car at a time to cross the dam. However when they saw all the beautiful Corvettes they let them all go at once. It really drew a crowd and everyone was taking pictures of the group. Now Dave and Maria belong to the North Idaho Corvette club, as well.

THE ROBERT WHITE FAMILY - San Diego, CA

For the White family, Chevy runs deep - about 40 years deep when it comes to Corvettes. Bob was 16 years old when his uncle bought a 1973 Canary Yellow Corvette and he vividly remembers borrowing the car for a first date --- because that date is now his wife Kim of 38 years. "That started it." Bob said, "From there my wife's father bought a 1978 25th Anniversary Corvette. That was his dream since he was a kid. Then my brother and I have each bought several Vettes since then."

The second generation of Vette ownership began with Dave's purchase of a 2000 Navy Coupe that was delivered to the Museum in August 1999.   This was quickly followed by Bob's first Corvette purchase a 1998 Black Coupe.

Adding to this stable of Vettes, the C5 was joined by a 1965 Red Coupe for his 30th wedding anniversary, then a 2006 Z06 (picked up at the Museum through the R8C Delivery program)., which he sold for a 2010 ZRI '65 Coupe, ZR1 & 78 25 Anniversary model.

Today, it's a 2015 Z06 with the Z07 package sitting in his garage -- a car he watched being built through the Museum's Buyer's Tour Program December 2015. Bob said, "I've been to the Museum many, many times. Our tour host was phenomenal, gave me a behind the scenes tour of the Museum. The Blue Devil had just been delivered (post sinkhole repair).

Bob, (on right) and brother Dave with the 2015 ZO6 being built behind them and a ZO7 up next.

Bob, starting his new car, right from the plant, with 0 miles on it.

The love of Corvettes has been passed down to the third generation when Bob's sons became owners as well. His son Ryan (32) now owns his Grandfather's 1978 Corvette. "My father-in-law is now 85 and he was going to sell it. We were like, "no way". It only had 45,000 miles on it and is in pristine condition. We gifted it to Ryan and he just loves it."

After upgrading the C5's with new C6s the White Brothers were off to Spring Mountain Driving School. "My brother and I went, literally, as it was opening up. We gave each other the three-day experience as birthday gifts. That was about ten years ago. They didn't even have the buildings yet and we watched them put up the first front gate. We've gone nearly every other year since. That turned Matthew to track. Bob's other son, Matthew, (27), has a 2003 Z06 that he tracks. And that hobby is all because of Spring Mountain.

Bob's son Matthew in a Z06 & Bob in ZR1 on the race track in 2003. Matt, is ahead!

Bob in the Spring Mountain red Corvette with son Ryan in the blue Corvette behind him

If you ask Bob why he keeps going back for more, he doesn't even hesitate with his answer. "It's just amazing to see the progress that we make. Every time I go it's better and better. The organization, the team, just the whole crew is professional. They still have a lot of the same people in place. They put together an outstanding program. The amenities, the condominiums and the drivers are focused on making sure you understand what good quality track time is. I keep coming back. Frankly, I think every kid should go through the defensive driving program. And, since Ron Fellows has been involved, getting to spend time with him is great. We'll be joining him at Mosport next year"

Bob, son Ryan and Ron Fellows at the Ron fellows, Spring Mountain Driving School

Bob's appreciation and enjoyment of high performance driving goes beyond his experience behind the wheel. He and brother David are Corvette racing enthusiasts, following the team to many races since the days of the C5-R. "I live in San Diego and my brother lives in Valencia. I would take my son and he would take his daughter and we would go to Laguna Seca, as well as Sonoma. It was a great time to spend with the kids. We saw the C7 R take laps under camouflage at Laguna Seca. We spend a lot of time traveling around the country, following the race team. - - - Road Atlanta, Long Beach, Sebring, the Detroit Auto Show, for the reveal of the C7R race car and the C7 Z06. That was phenomenal."

We are truly, truly a big Corvette family through thick and thin." Bob added.

The next photo shows Bob's family showing their cars at the San Diego, Plastic Fantastic Show, that attracts over 300 Vettes each year. Their cars are the '65 Coupe, '05 Convertible and the 2010 ZR1.

<u>DAN & SHIRLEY TWEED - Trail, B.C. Canada</u>

I was born in a small Canadian town in 1955.   Ever since I was a little guy, I had always had a passion for Corvettes. I remember growing up next door to my neighbor Tom, who had a 1963 split window and Booty Griffiths, an icon around our hometown of Rossland, B.C., who sold ski boots for Lange and drove a black 1965 convertible. I always knew that at some point I would own a Corvette.

I finished all of my schooling and entered the work force at the giant smelter in Trail, B.C. as an apprentice electrician and became a journeyman in 1978. I was single and had a stable job with great pay so it was time. In 1982 I found a 1971 LT1 Corvette Stingray in the Vancouver newspaper for $10,000. It was Bridgehampton Blue with a 350 cubic inch, 350 horsepower engine and a four speed trans, with black interior. It wasn't a highly optioned car, but to me at 27 years old, it was my dream car. It was love at first sight and I knew immediately the I was buying it!

The deal was done and I headed out on my 450 mile drive back to Rossland.   I was cruising along without a care in the world, feeling like a rock star when I got about halfway home and heard a horrific screeching noise coming from the back! I limped the car to Princeton, a small town on the verge of being a ghost town, due to the mines closing and found a garage.   The mechanic scratched his head as

he had never worked on a Corvette before, but it was the only show in town so I was committed. He took off the back wheels, pulled the rear brakes apart and as he dug deeper, he found that I had spun a bearing. I was lucky that the damage was limited to the actual bearing and that I hadn't seized everything up on my limp to town. Obviously there were no parts in the sleepy little town so he called a GM dealer in Vancouver and ordered parts. Three days later after going stir crazy in the one cafe, one motel, one bar town, the parts arrived on the bus and a few hours later I was back on the road headed for home.

I drove the car everywhere and always had a feeling of adrenaline rushing through my body when I got behind the wheel. A couple of years later, I was working in Yellowknife - way up north when I met my wife. She moved to Edmonton and I now live in Trail - a distance of 1000 miles. There were no cell phones, computers, emails or texting so I decided to make the drive and try to figure out if she "was the one." I drove to Edmonton and showed up at her front door in the Corvette to be greeted by her somewhat skeptical father who grunted derisively at me as he called his daughter to the door. We did however grow to be great friends.

I hung out in Edmonton for a few days, dating Shirley - she was definitely "the one" and coincidentally she had owned a 1966 and 1977 Corvette so that sealed the deal! One day while contemplating life on my way to meet her, I was driving down the freeway on the south side of town when a pallet blew off the back of a semi-trailer and before I could even react it was under the car. It tore off the oil pan and a piece of the pallet broke off and lodged up into the alternator and fan and took them out as well. So - - -there I was, stuck in another town waiting for repairs. A speed shop took pity on me and repaired all of the damage at a reasonable cost and I decided, what the heck - might as well throw a set of headers on while they were working on it. everything worked out in the end and Shirley became my wife in 1986. We bought a house that year and as newlyweds with a mortgage and high interest rates, finances dictated that the "toy" had to go.

I was sad because it had just been repainted and restored and it looked amazing. I was going to take it back to Vancouver and sell it on consignment at Corvette Specialties.   My Dad was going to follow us down and drive us back once the car was dropped off.   We were minutes away from leaving and as he swung his truck around the big step bumper on the back caught the rear quarter panel of the Stingray and opened it like a can opener. I was devastated.   after a lot of yelling followed by tears, we put duct tape on the fender to hold it together and even painted it blue so it was less noticeable.   We made the 450 mile drive and explained what happened at the dealer. We were only there about an hour with a broken car when the salesman came up and gave us a check for $20,000. Someone had walked onto the lot, saw the car and bought it instantly, in spite of the damage.

Some years later it changed hands again and the fellow called me to tell me he was taking very good care of my baby and said I could drop in any time for a visit.

The years rolled by. In 1993 I quit the smelter and started my own electrical contracting business and the economy was taking off so I never looked back.   Business was booming, we were comfortable settled in our house, all the bills and the mortgage were paid and we survived the impending doom of the new millennium so we decided maybe it was time for another Corvette. In 2001 I found a beauty in Phoenix, Arizona so I had it checked out at a Corvette dealership - it was a pin.   I also had a buddy in Vancouver that was the sales manager at a dealership so we bought the car and he had his broker import it for us.   It was a 2000 CF5 Corvette convertible with black and gray interior and every available option at that time. What a machine! We live in an area where we get four distinct seasons, one of which obviously is winter. In spite of the six months only that we could drive the car, we managed to put a lot of miles on the clock and I found hearted storage for our baby to keep her warm until spring.

We joined a local club and the Spokane, Washington Corvette Club and started attending car shows with other Corvette buffs. The car was beautiful and so easy to drive with all the modern conveniences that the '71 lacked.   As we hung out with more and more car nuts, the "need for speed" coursed through my veins and I made many trips over the years to the Champ Car and Indy races where I was fortunate to meet and have photos taken with the great Mario Andretti and Paul Newman. Life was pretty good!

We kept the 2000 convertible for many years until the C7s came out. This era for the car was amazing! I started searching on the internet and found a 2014 Stingray, 3LT, 6 speed automatic at a dealership in Kamloops, B.C.

It had a bit of a tragic story in that an elderly gentleman ordered the car from GM in March of 2014 and finally took delivery in September of that year. He only drove the car for two weeks and put it away for winter. In February of 2015 he passed away and the family took the car back to the dealership where I found it. I was turning 60 in June and I had recently retired so I thought I deserved a "present" for reaching the two milestones - - - We virtually made the deal over the phone and I drove up to Kamloops and bought the car. Now we had two Corvettes - his and hers!

This car was a beauty and I make a few refinements, adding a black stripe on the hood, a rear spoiler and some very subtle pinstripes to accent the additions. We drove this car and the convertible for the next year and once again put them away for winter. I had the "Corvette Fever" and in 2015 GM added the 8 speed paddle shift automatic and numerous other refinements to what I thought was already the perfect car. Over the winter I drooled over every Corvette publication I could lay my hands on and read every specification, option and review.

Summer of 2016 arrived, both cars were back on the road and I started looking on line once again. I called the same dealership and they told me they still had a brand new 2015 Z51, 3LT,460 HP, 8-speed automatic, electronic limited-slip differential, magnetic ride, heads up display, navigation system, dry sump -fully loaded, Daytona Sunrise Orange with 12 miles on the odometer and they were anxious to make a deal as the 2017s were just around the corner.

I listed the 2000 convertible on line and we got a call from a gal and her husband. They came and looked at the car and bought it on the spot so I took the cash and the 2014 as a trade-in and made an offer complete with a bumper-to-bumper 7 year extended warranty included and waited for their reply. We did the dance back and forth but I felt I had the upper hand as they really wanted to sell this car. I never moved from my initial offer and a week later while on the golf course, I got a text "Come and get your new car!"

We took the 2014 for one last drive to Kamloops and made the deal.

This car is the ultimate. It has every creature comfort known to an and goes like a rocket all while getting amazing gas mileage thanks the amazing GM engineering. Once again, I added a few refinements - a little carbon fiber here and there and some subtle stripes to accompany the "Jake" logo for Corvette racing that sits proudly on the hood.

I follow the C7R racing program and much to my delight, GM offered a subsidized session of high performance driving at the Ron Fellows - Spring Mountain High Performance Driving School in Pahrump, Nevada.

I contacted them and the car qualified for the program whereby you give them your VIN number and they put yo9u in the seat of an identical car in Nevada to learn every little detail about the car and how to drive it at high speed. I was like a kid in a candy store - Disneyland for adults! I arrive in Las Vegas and made the 45 minute drive to Pahrump and checked in. The program include instruction, 5-star luxury accommodation and meals and of course - new Stingray to drive.   All of the instructors and ex-race car drivers with backgrounds from sprint car, Nascar, off-road to Indy. They even have a professional photographer on site to capture the memories.

I started the course and was amazed at the intensity with which they taught.   we started out doing mundane ABS panic stops - akin to Mr. Miyagi on Karate Kid "wax on, wax off" progressing to exercises on dry and wet skid pads to the ultimate driving around the racetrack at speed. I got to make my "hot laps" rode along with a gal named Jennie Haraldson - ex Nascar driver and only dreamed of driving at that speed in spite of racing earlier in my life.   She said not to worry, "By the end of the course you'll be passing me."   I was one of the more aggressive drivers and the instructors told me after that I was welcome to back an bypass the Level One course moving directly to Level Two.   It was an amazing experience and I would recommend it highly to any Corvette owner that has an opportunity to attend. The skills that one learns are immeasurable even for every day driving. I'm already inquiring about the Level Two course dates!

While there we drove the School cars around the track.

The Ron Fellows Instructors and the folks that were my fellow class mates

Corvettes have pretty much been a part of me for my entire life. It's hard to explain the passion that one has for the manqué but it is amazing. Our Corvette Club is Spokane is gearing up for the "Glass on Grass," car show in late July - the 25th Annual, and rest assured --- I'm already polishing the car in anticipation.

We attended the "Glass on Grass" in Spokane, Wa. Had a great turnout of approximately 185 Corvettes on the lawn at Riverfront Park next to the river. This is a yearly event sponsored by the Spokane, Wa. Corvette Club.

The car show was followed by a barbecue at a park in Cheney, Washington, about a half hour drive so we all went out in a convoy, which turned a lot of heads. After dinner, we left to go back to Spokane and disaster struck… out of nowhere two deer ran out of the ditch and we heard a loud bang. One went over the roof of the car and the other took out the fascia, fender and headlight.

Deer Damage

I was devastated! I took the Corvette to our local body shop and they did an amazing job of fixing it with all new parts - $7000 damage. Now the question became, as much as I loved the car, could I live with it being broken? The answer was simply NO!

I set out on the internet looking at new 2017's and found a beauty in Sherbrooke, Quebec, Canada. I made a deal with our local dealer, Northstar GM and had the car transported out to BC. I picked it up and it was outstanding! The new Corvette was a 2017 Corvette Grand Sport Collector Edition Convertible! $125,000 sticker price - but this was the pinnacle of Corvettes for me. Absolutely fully loaded with exposed carbon fiber spoilers, side skirts, headrests - even the dash! It also came with the

Z07 performance package, which included the hand tuned suspension, Michelin Super Pilot cup 2 tires (essentially a street legal race tire) and carbon ceramic brakes. Brembo 6-piston 15.5" brakes on the front, 4-piston 15.3" on the rear. We took delivery of the car and the very first weekend we had it, we went to a big car show in Nelson, BC in which we took first place in our very first outing! Apparently we aren't the only ones in love with this car.

This is our baby now and as I write this, the days are getting shorter and colder so it means that winter is on the way and our baby will have to be put into hibernation until spring.

We are sad that we have to store the car after only being able to drive it for a month, but when we take it out in the spring, it will be a new Corvette with lots of miles in its future – that brings the smiles back to our faces!

PAUL & KATHY HERBOLD, - Bellingham, WA.

Jerry and I have been best buddies since 1958. We both bought 2012 Corvettes, me a torch red "Vet" and him a metallic red coupe. We are Corvette racing fans. We planned a road trip from Sandpoint, Idaho to Austin Texas to watch the Corvette racing team compete in the American LeMans Series at the Circuit of the Americas.

We had decided to take Jerry's car because my "vet" didn't have room in the cockpit for his oxygen machine (Jerry sustained severe lung damage while working for 3 months, "in the hole" during the recovery from the World Trade Center attack, and requires oxygen most of the time.)

I flew from my home in Bellingham, Wa. to Spokane where he picked me up at the airport. We departed for Texas the next day.

Our trip was run mostly at speeds between 90 and 100 MPH whenever conditions permitted. Jerry has a very good radar detector, but we saw very few highway patrol until we entered Kansas. There it seemed like they were everywhere we looked. We got safely past the first 11 without incident.

The road was 4 lane concrete, with a level grass median and no barrier separating the opposite lanes. It was a bright sunny day and traffic was almost non-existent. Jerry was driving at 100 MPH, when the radar detector suddenly went off. He nailed the brakes but the Patrolman, coming from the opposite directions had us at 90+MPH. Jerry headed for the shoulder to stop even before the Patrolman had turned around to follow us.

After stopping, Jerry got out of the car to converse with the Patrolman, leaving the engine running and me in the passenger seat. After about 5 minutes I shut off the engine and after about 10 minutes, Jerry finally got back into the car. I asked him what had taken so long. He said the first thing the Patrolman said was that he was not going to issue a citation. Then he asked for Jerry's driver license, which was in his wallet with his badge. (Jerry is a retired law enforcement officer). They talked some more and the Patrolman then said that he wasn't going to issue a written warning either.

Then Jerry asked the young officer if minded if he asked a personal question "off the record". After a slight hesitation the officer said, "No, I guess not." Jerry said, "Look, I am driving a 190 MPH car, the weather and the road are perfect and there is no traffic. Do you really think what I was doing was unsafe?" The officer scratched his chin, thought about it for a minute and finally said, "Well, I would worry about the tires." To which Jerry replied, "They are 200 MPH rated run flat Michelins, and I am a trained driver." After a moment to consider this, the officer said, "Well then, I guess not."

Jerry then asked the officer if he would mind doing him a favor. After another brief hesitation, the officer said, "Well, if I can." Jerry then asked if the officer would mind radioing ahead to tell his buddies that a couple of "good guys" were coming through and to "cut them some slack." The officer responded, "I'm pretty new on the force and I'm not sure they will do it, but ok." We parted ways and continued across the remaining part of Kansas.

Our last sight of Kansas, in the rear view mirror, was a Kansas Highway Patrolman standing beside his car with a radar gun waving his hat at us as we went by him at 100MPH. - - - True story.

In April of 2014, Cathy and I drove our 2012 Corvette Convertible to attend the American Le Mans Races at the Mazda International Raceway at Laguna Seca, California.

While we were there Cathy saw her first new series7th generation Corvette on display there. She and I both loved it, but we decided to wait for the 2015 model year.

We had put 30,000 miles on the 2012 in just 20 months and totally enjoyed it. It was the best car I ever owned, but if you know anything about the new 7th Generation model you would understand.

I ordered our 2015 Z51 Convertible in July 2014, even before pricing was available. We traded in our 2012 convertible on the totally redesigned new model and ordered it for Museum Delivery at the National Corvette Museum at the Bowling Green Kentucky Plant.

We bought very expensive non-refundable ($700 each) VIP Paddock Suite tickets for the American Leman's race at Circuit of the Americans in Austin, Texas. We ordered the car in July, but it had to be re-ordered in early August because the original order erroneously left out a very important option, (magnetic ride control). When the error was discovered, the car was already scheduled for production and it was too late to change the order.

It took intervention by my dealer, the GM Area Manager and a senior GM executive to get it re-ordered and produced in time to take delivery in conjunction with our trip to Austin.

On 9-2, The National Corvette Museum confirmed delivery for 10am on 9-23. Our plan was to proceed from the race in Austin on to the Corvette factory in Bowling Green KY, to enjoy the very special Museum Delivery Experience, so I immediately bought non-refundable one way airline tickets and made motel and rental car reservations for both legs of the trip, (Bellingham to Austin, Austin to Nashville, then drive from Nashville to Bowling Green.)

Then on 9-15, I read about the "Stop Sale Order" on the 2015 Corvettes. I immediately contacted GM and confirmed my car was affected. I contacted the Museum and they e-mailed me to inform me they could not provide any assurance the car would be delivered as promised due to the "quality hold" at the plant on the 1st 2000 of new 2015s.

Believing I had no other alternative, on 9-15, I cancelled the Museum Delivery and requested the car be delivered to the dealer. No one mentioned that GM had begun shipping Corvettes by rail, involving 3 loading and unloading cycles and up to a month in transit on 3 different railroad lines. Prior to the 1st of the year they all went by truck and were at dealers within a week.

I cancelled all the reservations for the Bowling Green part of our trip including non-refundable airline tickets and purchased round trip tickets from Austin on 9-23 to Bellingham.

Then, just before our departure on 9-17, I turned in my trade in and paid in full for the new car. While we were in Austin from 9-18 through 9-23, no one from the Museum followed up to tell me that the car could have been delivered no more than 2 days late. The quality problem was corrected and our car was actually shipped on 9-26. If I had only known, we could easily have spent a couple of extra days in Bowling Green, taken delivery of our car and enjoyed the trip home in it.

The car was uploaded from the rail car in Kent, Wa. at 12:30am Wednesday, 10-22 after sitting there unloaded for 6 days and was finally delivered on Friday, 10-24-'14. We insured, licensed and paid for the car and were without a 2nd car since September 17th, and we missed out on the once in a lifetime opportunity to enjoy the Museum Delivery Experience.

The process was like a very difficult pregnancy and birth. Once the mother holds that baby in her arms, all

the pain and suffering rapidly fades away.   I love this car and now have over 24,000 miles on it, but it is unlikely I will ever have a 2nd child.

FLO AND GRIPPER GRIPPO - Superior, MT

Here is a quick story on our 2006 Corvette. It was Christmas of 2005 that Grip had said to me that he always wanted a Corvette. So I went looking for a Vet to give him for Christmas. Well I found one. It was a yellow Barbie Corvette toy and presented him with his present. It sat on the window still in our garage for a year. It was the following Christmas that we were heading to Florida for our nephews wedding. On the way to the airport we received a call from Kyle Tyler Chevrolet that his corvette was in. All I heard him say was to keep it in the show room until May. At the time we were renting with no garage while our house was being built in Superior Montana.   After our return trip I was getting phone calls from friends stating that they saw our Corvette in the show room with Grippo's name on it.   I was in shock as hubby bought the vet without informing me. Well to make a long story short that was 11 years ago and yes were both thrilled owning our corvette.

We are "charter members" of the North Idaho Corvette Club from Coeur d'Alene, Idaho.

RON AND JOLENE MARTIN - Coeur D' Alene, ID

It was under unusual circumstances how the Martin's acquired their 1998 Corvette. It is the car Ron has always loved. They have had, over the years a 1957 T-bird and a 1979 MGB. About five years ago Ron and Jolene were at the Buick dealer in town for a service on one of their vehicles. Jolene sat in the lounge area with their miniature poodle, Dino. Ron was talking with Bill (a friend and salesman there) reminiscing about the good ol' days in San Francisco. Jolene spots a cute little 2008 silver and black Pontiac Solstice, same color as Dino. So while Ron and Bill were busy talking Jolene and Dino went into the manager's office and put their John Hancock on paper for the cute little 5 speed Solstice convertible much to the guys surprise. That was the easiest commission Bill ever made. Jolene and Dino took the car home and had a ball driving it around for weeks. Finally, one day Ron said he wanted to drive "Hottie". It turned out to be so funny just watching him try to get in the car. He finally made it. Knees under his chin and head up over the windshield. He drove it, but not very far. So much for Ron getting along with Hottie. As Jolene and Dino toured around the countryside Ron happened to mention to Bill that he couldn't get in Hottie (even though it was Jolene's car). One fine day in February after days of snow, Bill called and said to bring Hottie for an even exchange for a 1998 C5 Corvette. Jolene was hesitant, but gave in and took Hottie to trade for the Vette if it met their standards.

Just seeing the car, Ron immediately wanted the Vette. Jolene reluctantly give up the Solstice. They drove the Vette home. Hwy 95 was groomed nicely. No problem getting along Rockford Bay Rd. and Loffs Bay Rd. but now the fun began - - - when they turned onto their private road and started up the hill. The road was nicely groomed with only a few icy spots, but the Vette had summer tires and all of a sudden started sliding backwards, all the way back down the hill stopping in a snow bank at the bend in the road! There they sat. Jolene got on the phone and called for a tow truck to come and get them and take the car 1/4 mile up the road to their house.

About ten minutes later a neighbor on his way home stopped, got his shovel out and started digging out on Ron's side of the car. A few minutes later another neighbor on his way home stopped, got his shovel out and started digging Ron out too. A little while later another neighbor came by and took Jolene home. No sense of her sitting in the car freezing when she could be home in a warm house with a nice glass of wine. About an hour later the Vette arrived home and put away in the garage for the rest of the winter. Quite an ordeal for the Martin's for their first day with their beloved Corvette.

Since then they have spent many summer days taking the Vette out on back road runs for the day, going to St. Maries, Sandpoint, Rose Lake and lots of other little towns off Hwy. 95 south, stopping in different towns for lunch. They have been to Leavenworth, Wa. a few times with the Vette, staying in their favorite B & B. So far maintenance on the Vette has been about $1,000. a year. Jolene wanted louder pipes and Ron wanted new wheels. Ron said that in about ten years, it will be a brand new Vette. They say it's so well worth it with all the fun they are having.

STEVE AND COLLEEN CLEVELAND -Redwood Valley, CA

Steve and colleen Cleveland belong to the Corvettes of Lake County Club in Lakeport, California.

When we married in 2011, Steve owned two 2003 Corvettes.   One was for the street and the other for auto cross racing.   One day Steve asked me to ride along with him when he raced. I hated it. I was VERY scared! He then suggested I drive.   I was like, OH NO!!!   Knowing how much it meant to him, I decided to go for it. Who knew?? I loved it! I raced Steve's car until I got comfortable and then I bought my little red coupe. A 2000 Vet.

We were in Oregon on a Corvette gathering with 200 other Corvette owners, when I had the opportunity to try "Drag Racing." WOW, what a rush!! I even got the 2nd best time off the light. - Beginners luck. HA!

One day wee were loading up the cars in our stacker trailer, when the cable broke and my car shot out headed toward a small cliff over the river - - I ran along side my little red coupe, jumped in and put on the brake - - just before it went over the edge. Steve was in shock - as was I. I said "WOW, didn't know how much I loved that little red Corvette!

Unfortunately, Steve was diagnosed with two Cancers. We sold two of the cars, but still had the race car when he passed on December 7, 2016. It was all torn apart as Steve was going to make some changes to it. Our club voted to make us life time members, even though we would no longer own a Corvette. A Very Special Club! - - Then, two of the members, Martin Franusich (On the right) and John Yde (on the left) said they had promised Steve to help him put it back together. So - - the promise then went to me, when Steve died. I am so grateful. They did this because they love Steve and me and the love of being Corvette owners.

At Steve's memorial service the streets were lined with Corvettes in honor of his love of Corvettes. Even an officer of the Corvette Museum, at Kentucky attended and spoke about how responsible Steve was when he was in charge of leading a caravan of 200 Corvettes to the Corvette Museum in Kentucky.

I will always be a lover of Corvettes and will cherish the memories of Steve and me racing together. God blessed us with two year of racing, and making friends with other Corvette owners.

I am sure Steve has a BRAND NEW CORVETTE in Heaven. HA!

God Bless all the Corvette owners out there ! Special thank you to Martin Franusich . He sold Steve's Corvette to an auto cross racer for me.   Colleen Cleveland

---

SAM KALMUK - Welland Ontario, Canada
1964 Corvette GRAND SPORT

While I was restoring my '55 Corvette in 1990, I saw an ad in the Buffalo N.Y. paper for a '63 SWC Corvette (Tan/Tan) for sale. I ended up buying it and quickly refinished it, so that I could drive it around, while still restoring my '55. In 1992 I saw a few pictures of a Corvette Grand Sport for sale, and decided to look into "building my own Grand Sport". But, I knew that my wife would not go for the idea of 3 Corvettes in our 2 car garage, so the '63 Split Window Coupe had to go. So off I went to Carlisle to sell my '63. While there, I saw a couple of Grand Sport Roadsters for sale, and I knew that I had to have one - - - so the '63 SWC was sold.

By the way, the '55 Vette ended up being a "Show Car", and I did not drive it.

With those funds from the '63, I knew that I could build a Grand Sport, and started the search & investigation into building one. I checked with D & D, as well as Jeff Leach of Mid America Industries. Jeff was the most helpful and I ended up purching the "Glass parts from him to build my own Grand Sport. I had the Frame built locally, as I knew that we had the expertise here, instead of buying a frame from down south, in the States.

After talking to numerous friends who were in the Racing field, we found L & J Chassis out of Burlington to build my GS Frame, using the '90 Corvette suspension Points & '64 Corvette mounting points, as I used the '64 Vette tub as the main body components, with which to attach the GS front & rear clip. I had previously found/purchased a front & rear suspension from a '90 Corvette as the basis for the suspension unit for the Grand Sport. Once the Frame/suspension was assembled, we had to get the Body bonded together. So now, it somewhat looked like a Grand Sport Corvette, and was a rolling frame/body, but it needed a lot more work on it to resemble a real Grand Sport. I refinished the fiberglass over the Roll-bar, and started to sand & sand & wet-sand the body.

Initially the GS sat too high on the frame. So, I had to replace the front & rear C4 Springs with correct ones from Vette Brake Products, in Florida, so that it sat properly, since the vehicle only weighed 2300 lbs. By that time I had a 350 4 bolt V8 rebuilt, by my friends at the Balancing Act in St Catharine's to about 400HP, and I already had a Muncie 4 speed M22 Transmission. So with the GS body almost finished, Pepe, Vince, Alfie and I installed the Driveline into the Grand Sport on a Sunday afternoon.

I then got Darren from Zoro Mufflers in Welland to complete the SS exhaust from the Headers to the side pipes. We ran 2.5" collectors to 3" chambered side pipes to 2.5" SS tips. What a sweet sound that was, when we started that 350 engine.

Then came the Finishing of the body & Doors to perfection so the Paint could be applied with the George Wintersteen colors. Again, I consulted with numerous friends as to who to use. My old Painter Friend was too busy, so i decided to use Niagara Industrial finishers, of Niagara Falls, and Andrew did a fantastic job of setting the doors, finishing the body for paint and painting with base coat and clear coat --- Great Job Andrew.

When this was completed, I had to "Start the GRAND SPORT, to hear the rumble again, all with the help of Mike turner Jr. & Sr.. It was starting to come together - - -

With the paint completed, I had Roly Borgatti of RB Signs do-up the Racing Livery Decals and Numbers for the Grand Sport. Man, the GS changed entirely when the Decals were added!

To finish the Grand Sport, I added the American Racing Razor 17" Rims with tires. It was quite a chore to find the correct size and offset before deciding on the correct choice for the Rims & Tires to fill the wheel-well without rubbing on turns.

After a few years, I knew I wanted a Correct looking Rim and after lengthy search, I found the Legend series Gunmetal Alum Rims that I now have. Again, the rims changed the appearance, resembling the Original #002 Grand Sport.

Overall, it was a long, long project as I had collected the Chassis, 350 engine, Muncie M22 Trans and body parts from Mid American Industries. Once all the pieces were collected, it was more time (and $$$) to start building the frame, assembling the chassis, suspension, bonding the body, installing the driveline, painting

the body and installing the wiring harnesses etc - - -WHEW - - - tired already thinking about it! It took me many years (close to 10) to complete this GS and the Vette. I'll be DRIVING - - - -

For now, I enjoy Cruising throughout Niagara and Western New York, as well as attending a few Car Shows, and eventually, I'll get to Mosport and onto the track - - -

When all was said and done we got to show the GRAND SPORT at Toronto's Performance World in March 2009. It was well received by the crowd, especially many of the ol' boys who remembered the Grand Sports in the early "60s.

I know it's not an "Original Grand Sport", but then #002 sold for $7.25 million - - - EH!

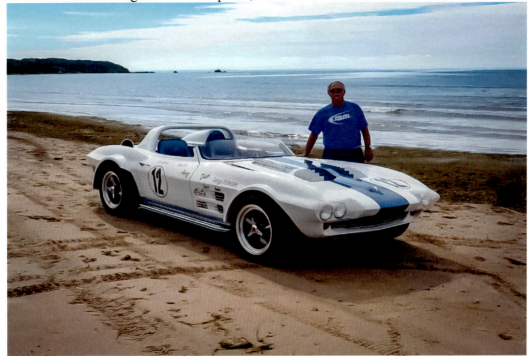

TRISTIN WANNER - Honolulu, Hawaii

Corvettes are beasts. And by beast I do not mean big, bulky, nor excessive; I mean they are chiseled and powerful yet elegant and dynamic. There is much to envy in a Corvette from its looks to its function.

For me as well as many others, the Stingray Convertible is the way to go. It is one of the highest performing sports cars on the market with all of the extra tools and gadgets to boot and an attention-grabbing design. This past summer I visited my Great Grandma Dale. While I was staying at her house, I had a fantastic time, though, one of my best times there was undoubtedly when for the first time in my life I was able to ride in a Stingray.

Every day when I passed the car in the garage I couldn't help myself but to sneak a peak; it was just the sharpest-looking car I had ever seen. Up until the day where I rode in the Stingray, cars were just about looks to me, but just a few seconds of being inside the Stingray and I knew that there was so much more to what makes a car great than what meets the eye. The car was smooth, it was fast, it was luxurious, and it simply felt right. "This is the car for me" was what I thought to myself as the rev of the engine sounded, the wind blew through my hair, and the seat held me comfortably. The ride felt amazing and the experience was grand.

The Corvette had a beautiful shiny, red paint, an interior built for royalty, and engine that can almost rival a super-car. Who wouldn't want a Corvette?

JOHN & BONNIE REMBER - Coeur d'Alene, ID

My husband John grew up with Corvettes as a part of his life. His Dad owned several, but John was never allowed to drive any of them, so I believe that there was always a desire in his heart to own one of his own.

A gentleman that he works with is the president of the North Idaho Corvette Club and was always putting a bug in his ear about buying one. Then one day he told John about someone in the club that was selling theirs, so John went and looked at it.

When he brought it home for me to look at my first response was, "My it is very yellow," but it is a beautiful car. I have very much enjoyed being a part of the North Idaho Corvette Club. I was really concerned how we would be accepted, because we bought it from a member of the club, but they have all been awesome to us and they have made us feel very welcome.

We have truly enjoyed the road trips that we have gone on this year and are looking forward to the years ahead with them.

Dave & Judy Van Hersett's 1964 Corvette History - Canada

Originally this was a 375 HP Fuel Injection Corvette. Over my wife's objections I purchased a stripped down piece of junk in 1974. My plan was to put it back together in its original condition. Well that has taken several years. At least my wife (girlfriend) knew where I was, in the garage working on the PROJECT. We drag race and autocross with it. Our four children took it to their High School Senior Prom. Many stories on those evenings.

My girlfriend of 58 years and wife for 54 years always says to me at the stop light, do not let those kids beat us! Thus we have replaced the engine four times with ever increasing horsepower. Cannot let those kids beat us. The latest engine is near 500 HP. We have replaced five rear-ends with the help of the neighbor high school boys and sons. They all know how to use a wrench, etc.

The current engine is a 383 cubic inch small block Chevy, Willwood disc brakes all around, a 5 speed, transmission, Dragvette 6-Link rear suspension system, special ring & pinion gears and power steering. These were installed by Pro-Automotive here in Spokane. A very fun car to drive and test your stop light skills.

Now we have six grandchildren and this gives Grandpa another ten years of racing with the kids. Great fun and creates great memories.

We take many road trips with the Vette. There is room for two sets of golf clubs, one large suitcase, and two small cases for my wife. Great fun. We are currently on the third air conditioner, a requirement to keep my girlfriend cool.

We hope this brings back memories for you all. Fondling is not allowed, finger prints you know. Enjoy!!!!

In 1974 I purchased a completely stripped 1964 FI Corvette Roadster. Drove it home sitting on a milk box. Refer to Photo's. Spent the next two years scrounging parts to put the car back together. Found two bent convertible frames and made one that works. After two years it was drivable and painted red with an all black interior and wire wheels. Note that the rear wheel well was rounded out as we liked that look then.

Joined the Spokane Corvette Club to find sources for parts. Then participated in club events of drag racing and autocross for several years. Finally located two Fuel Injection units. One installed on the Vette and sold the other several years later. Should have kept the fuel injection unit longer. Ran with the FI for 20 years. Finally had to switch to a carb to have the reliability that my wife wanted. She drove the Vette often. Another reason was that the soft plug on the side of the fuel pump came off and squired a ½ inch stream of gas onto the exhaust manifold. I was driving on 1-90 Freeway, coming back to Spokane from Coeur d'Alene and smelled gas in the car. Turned off the freeway at Freya and went to the Standard station on Sprague. I opened the hood and saw fuel squirting a stream about thumb size onto the exhaust manifold. then the flame reignited and the gas station operator came running out with his big extinguisher and put out the fire in the engine compartment. My Halon extinguisher ran out of gas. Very lucky that the Vette did not burn to the ground. Fiberglass makes a very good fuel. A close call, this is a strong testimony to carry an extinguisher in your car at all times. I have two extinguisher in my car at present.

Had to rewire the engine compartment and replace all the rubber hoses. Refiniisyhed all aluminum parts such as the Fuel Injection unit to place my car back into service and running.

Early modifications made were to support autocross activities. Fabricated a Heim joint front and rear sway bars. These worked very well and gave the Vette a neutral steering. Switched to the quick steering position on the steering rods. For racing tires used worn snow tires that had a stickey seal. On a budget these worked great.

Over the years our four kids helped with the maintenance and repair to the Vette. They all helped install replacement rear ends, half shafts, tires and oil changes. Good training for their after life.

In 2010 we were ready for a new paint job. So we went to the Spokane Corvette body shop operated by Tom Fisher. He did an excellent job taking the parts off the car and doing it right. We replaced the real panels to have a stock appearance. However this Vette is a real animal. The interior, instruments, seats, etc. are all stock. Subtle mods were made to make the Vette "streetable" and reliable for long road trips.

For Cooling we installed an aluminum radiator with an independent thermostat for an electric fan to keep the max temp at 180 deg. Thus no problems with parades or hot weather. Sway bar upgraded for front & back using poly bushing for flat cornering. A Brogenson Power Steering 12:1 for smooth and fast response at autocross as well as easy for the driver. The latest engine is a 383 Stroker Engine by Ron Prior, Pro Automotive, Spokane.

I purchased my 1962 Corvette Roadster in mid July of 1966, after my tour of duty from Naha, Air Force Base, Okinawa. I am the third owner. The original owner ordered and purchased it from a dealer in Willits, Ca. picking it up in December 1961. I know it's whole history.

The car was not in very good shape after all the drag races it went through. Blown 327 ci/ 360 hp engine, (twice,) has a sleeve in #7 cylinder, blown rear gears and the T-10 kept jumping out of gear on compression. The owner also replaced the Fuel Injection with a four barrel Carb. I have no idea how many miles were on the 62 Corvette when I bought it. It was really not that important then. Besides the speedometer was not working. Hah !

Since it was my only mode of transportation, I used it for camping on the Eel River, catching breakfast, lunch, & dinner. Just enjoying my freedom for a few months till I ran out of money and had to go to work.
I purchased a ski 'HOT' boat that weighed three thousand pounds and was pulling it with my
three thousand pound Corvette.   (Still have the tow bar & ball mounted on the 62 but not pulling boats anymore.)

A Mural is painted on the Little Lake, NAPN Auto Parts Store in Willits with my 62 Corvette.

I have been a Charter member of the Shifters Car Club from 1958, restarted back up twenty years ago, and now am the only active member left in the club. I am a member of several other Corvette Clubs, as well, Solid Axle Corvette Club. International, and NWSACC, of (Washington State). Western States Corvette Council Wine Country Corvettes, (NAPA) Corvettes of Lake County, (Charter member & President four times) Corvettes of Sonoma County, Club Corvette Denmark (E mail member)

Through the years the "62 ALL WEATHER" Roadster, has never been "trailered" or wrecked and drives in the snow, rain. It taken many awards when entered in "Corvette" shows, as well as "all car" shows. I do all my own work and it has never been in a shop.

In 2011 it was awarded first place for the year and the most traveled that same year, from the WSCC.

In 2012 it was awarded second place in the Sacramento Autorama, (old Oakland Roadster Show)

Have driven it in 37 High School Home coming games, many parades, including the "Vets in Vettes" parade in Petaluma, on Veterans day. as well as driving laps at the Laguna Seca race way in 2002. (SACC), Thunder Hill, and Sonoma Raceway.

A True
"Rosie the Riveter"
Worker
Lee Chappat
Marinship - Sausalito, Ca.
Arc Welder
At Age 17!
'42 '44
Driver: JOHN YOE CORVETTE

This is. Ms. Lee Chappat, from Sausalito, Calif. One of the original "Rosie the Riveters". I was privileged to drive her in the "Vets in Vettes" parade for two years. She was 90 yrs old the first time and 91 the second. Sadly, she passed away last year.

Have rebuilt the engine twice, installed a TKO 600 five speed transmission, still running 4:11.1 posi. rear gears, painted it four different colors, (on was Hugger Orange, then mostly Purples), running 255X60X15 BFG tires, LED lighting, Halogen headlights, Mallory Ignition, with 367,000+miles on the '62 that I have put on, still the original KING pins. And am a member of the Mike Yeager's "High Mileage Club".

Western States Corvette Council Convention at Fallon Naval Airbase in Reno, Nevada,

On a trip we got this '05 Orange Vet and this '59 Corvette (go-cart) with a 3 hp. Briggs & Stratton engine. for our son Erik when he was five. It has been in lots of parades. - - He is now 32 and we both still drive it.

Erik, working on his Corvette

Gail, out for a drive

I am now working on a '65 Corvette Coupe for the 40 year old son of the father who also passed away.   It has been setting for forty years.   Only thing that worked was the radio. Doing a complete overhaul. It is now all apart and I'm starting to put it back together again.   Then will paint - - --- - - -

65

My seven car garage and workshop

ED AND JOANNE CHEROSKI - Ontario Canada
How I Survived a Sharkbite

I've had a thing for Corvettes since I was twelve years old. My first ride in a Vette was in my brothers 58. I just loved the way it sounded and the feeling as he shifted through the gears. I was hooked. All I had to do now was grow up, get a job, save some money and maybe someday...

Well they say "you are where you are because of the choices you made". So true. Add to that a coincidence or two and life takes off in its own direction. For me, the coincidence came first. That might be easier to understand if I start at the beginning. Things seemed to be working out as planned. I grew up, got a job and even saved some money. My first real job out of high school was working for a local boat manufacturer. My job description was "fiberglass laminator/chopper gun operator". We built yachts ranging from 24' to 54'. That's a boatload of fiberglass! I didn't realize at the time how significant learning to work with these materials would be.

After working for about a year I started thinking about buying a new car. It was the winter of 1976/77, the year of Smokey & the Bandit and I had my eye on a shiny new black Trans Am, until I got a call from my older brother Mike. "*Hey, I'm selling my Vette...You interested*? Hmm, another coincidence? I gave it some serious thought for maybe three seconds! "Yah, I'm interested. I soon became the proud new owner of my first Corvette, a 1972 Mille Miglia red on black big block with all the options of that year. The unfortunate thing though, it was early winter and up here in Ontario Canada, that meant about 3 feet of snow for the next 3 months. The car took up residence in my parent's driveway.

I would go out and fire it up every few days just to here it rumble. Man that was a long winter. When the snow finally melted, I wasted no time hitting the road, and hit it I did. I had only been driving the car for about a month when it happened. Now you have to realize this was over forty years ago and I was young and foolish...no, make that *downright stupid*! I really wanted to know how *fast* this thing would go, so late one night I headed out to the country where there was a long stretch of road. When I was satisfied there were no cars in sight I let her rip. I remember glancing down at the speedometer...125, wow! Just as I looked up, headlights were coming at me and I guess it must have startled me. I hit the brakes. Big mistake at that speed. I learned a hard lesson in Corvette suspension geometry and as you might have suspected, the rear end passed the front end. I was in for the longest twenty second ride of my life. I wiped out nine guardrail posts, one hundred and fifty feet of farm fence, then cart wheeled six or seven times down a thirty foot embankment where it came to rest on its side, no more than ten feet from a creek. I crawled out of the wreck and walked away basically unharmed. The car had completely disintegrated.

Once the dust had settled, I made the decision to get back into another Corvette. Knowing that my insurance would triple for the next few years, my plan was to find a car, drive it until late fall then put my fiberglass skills to work building a custom. Within a month I purchased a 1969 small block coupe and enjoyed *safe* driving for the rest of the season. I got together with a couple friends and we rented a small shop where we could work on our cars. I got right to work tearing down the car, striping the paint, building flares and spoilers and anything else I could find a way to change. Friends would stop by the shop to check on the progress and before long they're asking me, "so when are you going to do my car?"

I've done plenty of fiberglass work before but I had never actually painted a car yet. I do need some practice, how hard could it be? I had been watching my brother do bodywork and paint since I was a little kid, so naturally I accepted the challenge. The first car I ever painted was a 72 Corvette coupe. It was dark blue with some 70's type graphics and it turned out great! It wasn't long before another one showed up, then another and another...I only had a three year lease on the shop but I had gotten plenty of practice before I finally found time to finish my own car. It was a real head turner when it was done. In fact I used it as my *rolling resume* and actually got hired doing prep and paint at a local custom shop. It didn't hurt that I knew a thing or two about fiberglass as well.

This was the beginning of another journey in my life that has stretched over forty years and counting. I had worked for a few different shops over the years and even tried different career paths but somehow I always ended up back in a body shop. I was building cool cars for customers while my own ride, a mildly customized 79 just wasn't cutting it.

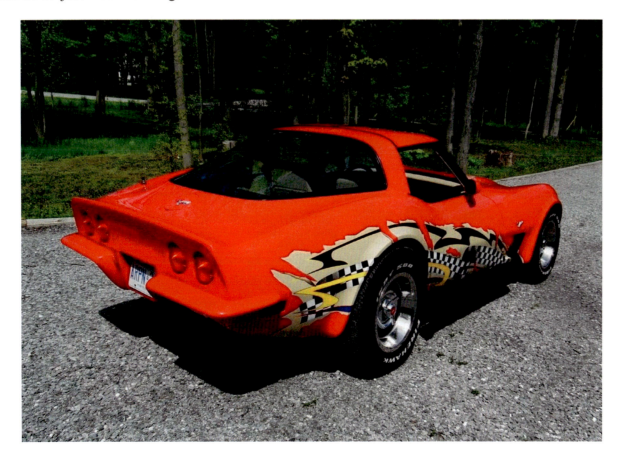

It seems that's just the way it goes in this business. You fix *everyone else's stuff* before you get to your own. I wasn't getting any younger so I decided it was time to build a car for myself! I knew that this would be a costly undertaking, so my plan was to try to flip a car or two just to generate some cash.

The search was on for a project car and being so familiar with C3 Vettes, I figured I would stick with what I know. Late in the summer of 2010 I found what I thought to be the perfect candidate, a 1973 coupe that had already been disassembled and stripped.

I knew the car had some birdcage issues around one of the body mounts but everything appeared to be relatively solid. Once I got the car home and started removing fiberglass to get at the rust damage I came to realize I may have made a huge mistake. The rust was far more extensive than I was able to see with the body panels in place. My heart sank. This thing is *JUNK*!!!

I considered parting it out, cut my losses and move on. After breaking the bad news to my wife, I called my good friend Kevin who was going to help with the mechanics of the build. He and my wife convinced me that it was worth saving.

Now the search was on for parts and to put together a plan as to just how far I would go with it.

Well we all know that plans change and it didn't make sense to go through all this work to sell the car. I decided this would be *my new ride*! I tore the car down to a bare shell and started from the ground up.

For the most part, the majority of the work was done by myself in my own garage at home, with the occasional trip to Kevin's house for fabricating and mechanical stuff that was beyond me. We made a deal that I would do the body work and paint on his Vette in return for his help with mine. Free labor...it doesn't get any better than that! Of course that meant my car would once again get set aside while I worked on his. *Some things never change*.

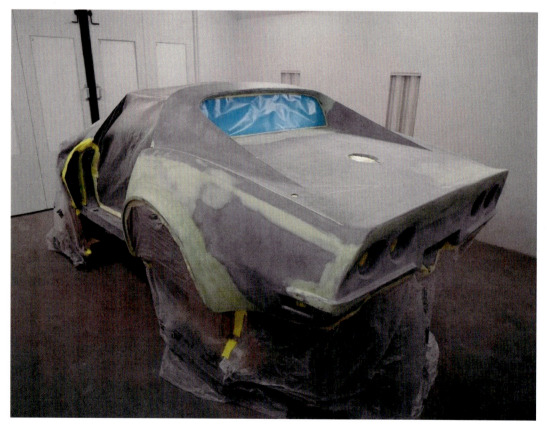

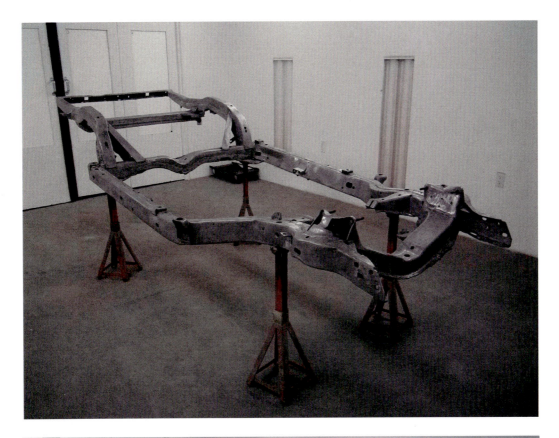

In time and as cash became available it came together piece by piece. All new aftermarket suspension, rack and pinion steering, tubular control arms, coil over shocks at all four corners and a complete new Willwood brake system.

The engine is a rebuilt and slightly modified 5.7 liter tuned port backed by a 5 speed transmission. While Kevin was keeping busy with the assembly of the rolling chassis, I was doing my fiberglass magic on the body, working on the under body, filling all the factory seams, smoothing everything over and getting it ready for finishing in candy gold as had already been done to the frame.

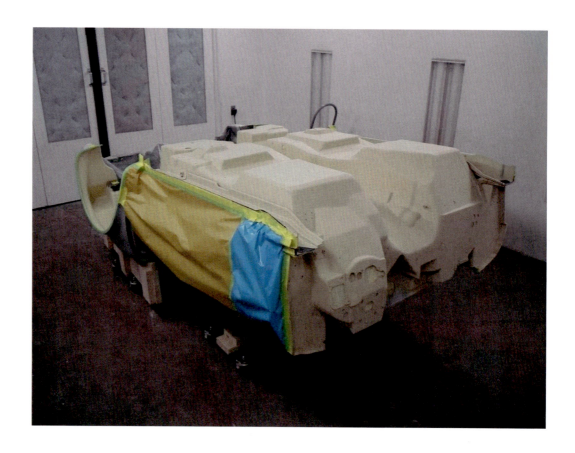

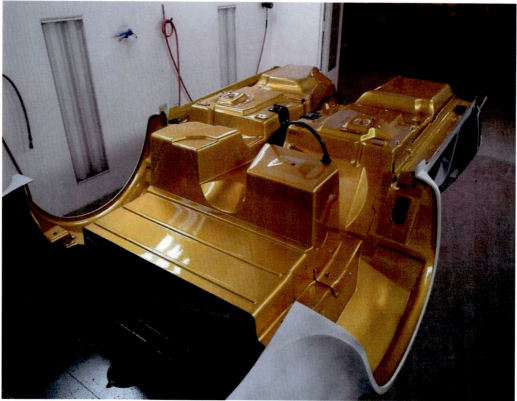

I remember one of the most exciting days being the day I dropped the body back on the chassis after nearly three years. I kept telling myself that one day all those parts sitting on shelves would once again occupy the same parking space.

It was at this point that I decided it was time to retire from the body shop business. For the next twelve months I focused my attention on getting this shark back on the road. Countless hours of block sanding, shooting primer and more blocking. Then it was on to paint. The graphics were laid out using marble FX overlaid with an assortment of pearls, metallic and candy black stripes all covered in candy gold. Next, a dozen coats of candy red over a custom blended ground coat then finished off with multiple coats of clear. Now on to my favorite part, sanding and polishing.

Finally a light at the end of the tunnel, the build was complete, the last part put in place, the last bolt tightened...victory and "Sharkbite" was born.

We have enjoyed cruising and attending car shows and cruise nights for two seasons now. It gets plenty of attention where ever we go and has won several awards. The end result was definitely worth the four years I spent in the garage.

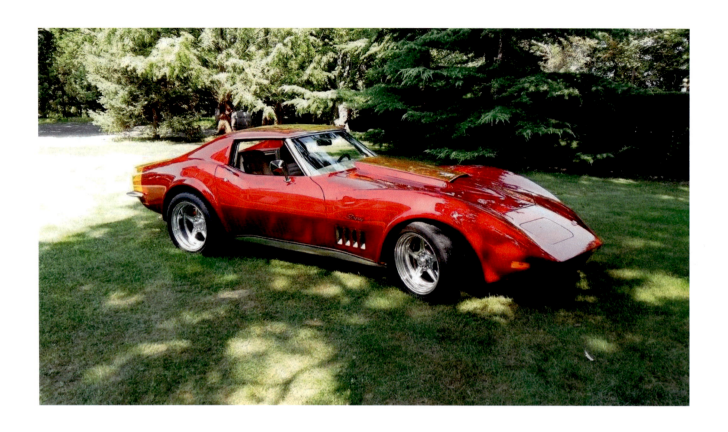

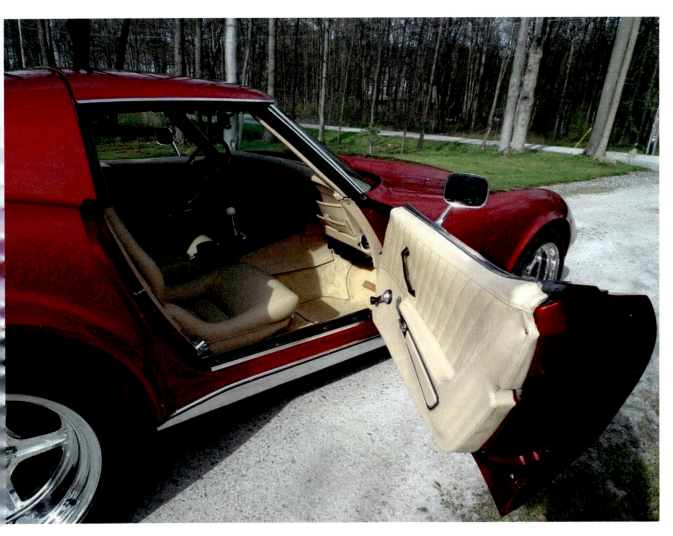

Many thanks to my wife Joanne for her encouragement and knowing when to leave me alone in the garage, also my good buddy Kevin Boverhof for all he did to help make this car a reality. As expected, friends are still asking "so when are you going to do my car?"

So there you have it, my forty year journey with Corvettes, once bitten by a 72 shark and lived to tell the story. Forty years of customizing, restoring and painting, all as a result of a wild twenty second ride and the desire to customize my own car. For forty years I've wondered what became of that twisted, mangled wreck. While writing this story and looking for photos, I found an insurance slip for that car which of course includes the VIN. I had the MOT search the number and was blown away by what they found. It had been purchased by an auto wrecker then sold to an auto body shop who, over the next two years were able to rebuild it! The last registered owner of the car has owned it for thirty five years. It still wears the same license plate it had when I owned it. I have the owners name but as of this time, have not found them......Yet!
Cheers and a friendly Corvette wave.   Ed Chernoski

Later note * - Dale, I just had to tell you this. I just spoke to the woman who now owns the 72 Corvette that I crashed! The car is in storage for the winter but she said I can come see it in May. I've wanted to know what happened to that car for 40 years and probably would never have looked if I hadn't written that story. I guess it was time. After owning it for 35 years, she has no idea about the cars history. This should be interesting.
Thanks for the opportunity.   Ed Chernoski

LANA AND DAN RODLIE - British Columbia, Canada

Wanna go for a ride?
By Lana Rodlie

 I never imagined when we bought our first Corvette that it would change our lives as much as it has. Being white-haired baby boomers, we got some pretty strange looks from folks. Our grown-up kids' reaction was "They bought a what!?"A 2014 Corvette Stingray 3LT Z51 Coupe, Torch red body with Adrenalin Red interior, Z51 Sport handling package with every option,7-speed manual transmission, 6.2L direct-injection (V8 376 ci), 455 hp @6000 rpm, 460 lbs.-ft. Torque, Carbon fibre hood and removable roof, Michelin Pilot Super Sport ZP Run Flats with Glossy Black aluminum wheels Head-up color display for street and track mode.

We took our black C6 coupe, which we dubbed "Black Rose," on the run to Bowling Green in 2014. In 2016, we traded it in for a red C7 coupe. The license plate still reads BLK ROS however, since the licensing department in British Columbia has so far refused to let us change it.

Anyway, we joined the Spokane Corvette Club because Spokane is just two hours south of us and there were no Corvette clubs in B.C. close to us. We now have dozens of American BFFs who we have traveled with to car shows and two more extensive caravans.

After the Bowling Green venture, we all wanted to get together again, so in 2015, we took a circle tour (12 cars) down the Oregon and California coast across Death Valley and up to the Grand Canyon, Yellowstone, finishing at the Big Sky Corvette meet in Bozeman, Montana.
This was such a great adventure, we wanted to do it again, and so we talked our American friends into coming north to Canada. My husband and I took a year to organize the tour, which we enjoyed immensely in September 2017.

For any group wanting to do this, I'm including the itinerary plus the hotels where we stayed. You could do any part of this trip – all of it, a week of it, or even just a few days of it, coming or going. Pick a time of year between May and September as a lot of museums and special attractions are closed during the Canadian winter (October to April).

A couple of things to note: we chose hotels that were generally top-of-the-line but not luxury – Holiday Inns, Hilton, Travelodge. The prerequisite was to make sure the parking lots were all Corvette-safe – no dirt, no speed bumps and lots of room to park together where possible.
Make sure to call the hotels directly – don't use the 1-800 numbers to a central registry as you can't book groups through there. Most hotels will want a contract signed for groups. Prices were ranged from $100 to $280 Cdn and most included breakfast. But the prices could be better than in 2017 as it was Canada's 150th birthday and hotels were taking adventure of the onslaught of "Canada 150" tourists.
Another thing we highly recommend is make sure someone has a list of all the contact people (next-of-kin) of all the folks on the trip. This is just for medical emergencies or (god-forbid) a car accident. We are all good friends, but we don't all know who we'd contact if the unthinkable happened.
I've highlighted the names of the museums and attractions we visited. Google them for more information.

The Grand Canadian Caravan
DAY 1 – Spokane, Washington, 15 cars: two cars from B.C., one from Montana, two from Arizona (friends of friends who heard about the trip and joined us) and the rest were Washington cars from the Spokane area. It was a great mix with more than half being C7s and even a mint 64' with over 300,000 miles on it.

We drove to our first stopover, the Holiday Inn Express, 275 Treeline Road, Kalispell, Montana, (call 406 755-7405). Since we got there fairly early in the day, we hit the road and drove up to **Whitefish**, an interesting little town with some neat bars and restaurants.

DAY 2 – Left Kalispell and drove over the **Going-to-the-Sun Road Highway**. Since this highway is closed for much of the year, it was a real treat, although we were starting to see the smoke of upcoming forest fires in the north. Once into Canada, we drove into Waterton, Alberta. Make sure to get a Discovery Pass which covers all 80 Canadian national and provincial parks. http://www.commandesparcs-parksorders.ca/webapp/wcs/stores/servlet/en/parksb2c/discovery-pass

Or just Google, Canada parks Discovery Pass.

Waterton National Park is the Canadian side of America's Glacier National Park. The small town of Waterton is a mini-tourist hub with quaint shops and plenty of places to eat along a beautiful lake and picturesque mountains. Parking is a bit difficult, but if you drive right down the main drag, you can usually find spots along the road – just an easy block or two from the downtown center. There is a lake cruise there, if you want to take the time. We gave ourselves a little over an hour to eat and shop. On the way to Lethbridge, we passed through Cardston, which is Mormon Central. We stopped at the **Remington Carriage Museum,** which houses the largest collection of horse-drawn vehicles in North America – over 270 carriages, buggies, wagons and sleighs. Follow the signs through town to get to it. Cost is $11 per person Canadian. There is a 20 per cent discount for groups of 15 people. From Cardston, make sure to keep on Hwy 5 to Lethbridge.

We arrived at our hotel in Lethbridge around 5 p.m. There are a number of good hotels, some bigger and maybe even nicer in the same area by the intersection of Hwy. 3 and 43A St. We chose Quality Inn and Suites, 4070 Second Ave. S., call 403 331-6440. Group rate was $109 Cdn. They went out of their way to provide parking all together – a major concern for us as we didn't want to be parked next to big trucks or other vehicles that could park too close. Most of us headed for the brewery across the street but some went to the nearby casino (both within walking distance so no need to move the cars.) The Quality staff treated us like we were the first people to stop there in 100 years. They bent over backwards to make sure everything was perfect – even called our rooms to let stragglers know which bar their friends went to.

DAY 3 – We were up early and headed back down Hwy 3 towards Fort McLeod to the Picture Butte exit (Hwy 25), a small town about 30 minutes from Lethbridge. We stopped at the **Prairie Tractor and Engine Museum/Coyote Flats Pioneer Village.** When you get to Picture Butte, you have to take the very first street to the right just as you enter town. Follow the signs. Some of our travelers thought this place was the highlight of the trip. It's basically a small old town with a railway station, post office an ice cream parlor (really good ice cream) and various blacksmith shops, a church, school and even an old jail. These buildings and hundreds of farming artifacts were collected over a period of time. If you go, be sure to see the Eaton House. This was a house people could buy from the Eaton's Company catalogue and have shipped to the prairies where it could be erected quickly, providing all the amenities of a modern home (in the early 1900s). What was most miraculous is: the volunteer historical society which runs the museum has decorated this house exactly as it would have been in its heyday. The furniture is pristine, the lace curtains were all "bleachy" WHITE and the entire place was a walk back in time. The school looks like kids and teachers had just left for recess. Cost was a donation (about $5 Cdn) and they welcome tours. Open end of May to September and closed Mondays, but they are very open to making exceptions. (We arrived on a Monday) Call first 403 732-5451. (They hold a classic car show every Canada Day weekend (July 1). Check the date before you go – last year it was July 2.

Our object when leaving Coyote Flats was to make it to lunch at a place called Wayne which is just outside Drumheller. We drove up the highway and stopped for gas at Vulcan. We had no Star Trek fans with us so we didn't go into the little "space museum" there but it may be worth a stop, if interested.
The Corvette club in Calgary, Alberta, recommended this side-trip to Wayne because the road is through a section of the Alberta Badlands which takes travelers over 11 bridges – once noted in the Guinness Book of Records as the most bridges in the shortest distance (6 kilometers). – THINK METRIC – YOU'RE IN CANADA.

Getting to Wayne is a little twitchy to find. Your GPS will try and lead you across a corn field and onto dirt roads, so don't trust it. There are no dirt roads on this trip, so if you find yourself on one – YOU'RE GOING THE WRONG WAY. (And yes, we know this by experience.) The attraction at Wayne is the **Last Chance Saloon**, a small bar and grill which is immensely popular as a tourist hole. But take away the word "tourist" and yes, it's pretty much a hole. But an interesting one. We booked ahead for lunch, to save time. 403 823-9189. You could get pretty filled up for $15 Cdn.

The next major stop was the **Royal Tyrrell Museum** which houses one of the world's largest displays of dinosaur artifacts. Open mid-May to end of September, cost $18 CDN. Rates are less for seniors. The exhibit is astounding with hundreds of examples of dinosaur bones and full skeletons as well as a peak at paleontologists at work. You could easily spend days there.

If you take more time, you can drive to Dinosaur Provincial Park, which is situated in the Badlands. There is an interpretive centre there but it is about an hour from Drumheller. We were told if we had to make a choice, do the museum.

There aren't a lot of hotel choices in Drumheller, so book early. We stayed at the Canalta Jurassic Hotel, 1103 Highway #9 South. Phone 403 823-7700. Cost was about $190 Cdn. I cannot recall where we had dinner, but there were a lot of fast-food places near the hotel.

DAY 4 - We timed our morning drive so that we could arrive early at the **Reynolds-Alberta Museum** in Wetaskiwin when it opened at 10 a.m. This is the largest car exhibit in Canada featuring a one-of-a-kind 1929 Duesenberg Phaeton Royale Model J and the world's oldest dragline – a Bucyrus Class-24. The exhibition gallery takes visitors along a "highway through time" from horse-drawn carriages from 1916 through four seasons of the year including a 1911 factory, a 1920s grain elevator, a 1930s service station and a 1950s drive-in. Besides the eye-popping vehicles we saw, some of our "caravanners" took rides in an open cockpit biplane.

We spent about four hours at this museum and then took on the longest drive of our tour – almost four hours, to Hinton Alberta. We chose to stay in Hinton, rather than the higher tourist-rated Jasper. Hinton is only about an hour away and much cheaper. Lakeview Inn and Suites, 500 Smith Street, phone 780 865-2575; cost $158 Cdn. This hotel had some double loft-rooms with two baths, if people wanted to share. While some rooms were "okay" some were really nice. We had a lovely large room with separate bedroom. A 10% discount for hotel guests in the restaurant next to the hotel.

DAY 5 – The highlight of this day was driving through **Jasper and Banff National Parks**. Stopping in all the places is almost impossible when you have 15 cars all wanting to stay together. The best way to hit everything or even just the highlights is to get a tour. Google **Brewster Canadian Rockies Tourist** info. Don't bother trying to find another tour company, you won't. You need to take a bus if you want to go to the Columbia Icefield or the Glacier Skywalk as you can't just drive to them. Check out the website as there are various prices for all the different tours.

We stopped at the **Columbia Icefield Discovery Centre**. It is a very long hike up to the main building from the parking lot, but you can actually drive on a road behind the parking lot that will take you up, if you have people who can't walk it. You can get tours to the Icefield from there but plan to say several hours. We stopped for lunch and then headed on down to Banff.

It was impossible to get into Lake Louise unless you parked 10 miles down the highway on a gravel road and took the shuttle bus up to the lake – unless you arrive very early, or at the very end of the day. Some of our "caravanners" went back the next day. We skipped it as the smoke from the forest fires was spoiling all the scenery anyway.

About Banff. First, try not to arrive there on a Tuesday or a Saturday. Those are the days that the Rocky Mountaineer train comes into town and tourists stay overnight. Hence, getting a hotel room on these nights is near impossible in high season.

Hotels are outrageously expensive but you can skirt them by staying in Canmore, east of Banff, or Golden in the west. Both cities are about an hour away. However, we didn't find prices much better in Canmore, and since we were going west, we made our second night stop in Golden. Ditto for Jasper. Hinton, in the east, is much cheaper and only an hour or so away. If coming from the west, Valemount is maybe two hours, but much cheaper than Jasper.

Also, must warn that hotel operators in Banff are not to be trusted. We had booked in November (10 months in advance) for our group for two nights but when we called to confirm our reservation in February, they said they didn't have it. We really had to scramble then to find a place to stay. When I called other hotels in Canmore and Golden, I learned that Banff hotels dumped their group bookings once the government announced the Canada 150 thing because they could charge more.

We ended up booking with Banff Park Lodge for one night and spent our second night in Golden. Cost was $259 Cdn., no breakfast included, but great underground parking.

Banff is Tourist Central and gridlocked most of the time. You really can't drive around there. Find a hotel, park it and take a tour. We booked a group tour with Brewster for Banff and area. The only downside was: we had to collect money from everyone in advance to get the group booking rate and all on the same bus. We did this months in advance as tours are premium for larger groups.

The tour was terrific though – about six hours. Cost about $145 Cdn per person. The hotel let us leave our cars in its parking garage after we checked out as they didn't need the spaces until late afternoon. The bus took us to all the best places to see: **The Bow River Falls**, a gondola ride to the top of the mountain and a cruise on glacial **Lake Minnewanka**, where you definitely don't want to fall overboard – even with a life jacket. The icy water will immediately drag you down into the depths.

Tom and Carrole Helman at Takakkaw Falls, Yoho National Park

We left Banff in late afternoon and drove to Golden, stopping at the three tunnels viewpoint (where you can see trains weaving through the mountains in Yoho National Park and Takakkaw Falls. The falls are only open mid-June to October and are one of Canada's highest. Although it's about a 20-minute drive off the highway, it's worth it. The road is windy with a few scary switchbacks but it's all paved.

Three tunnel view, Yoho National Park - Smoke from the fires spoiled our view somewhat.

Yoho has some beautiful lakes and hiking trails, if you want to explore. This is through the Rocky's Yellowhead Pass which is a very treacherous highway most of the year so drive carefully. You'll likely hit road construction through there as they are always fixing parts of it.

At Golden, we stayed at the Travelodge Golden, 1200 12th Street, call 250 344-2915. Price was $172.50 Cdn. (I made a note on my hotel receipt – "best sleep ever, great room temperature, good room, very clean and there is a great Chinese and a BBQ restaurant nearby to walk to."

DAY 6 There wasn't much of a drive from Golden to Kamloops – our next sleepover, so we made use of the time by stopping at some of the venues along the way. The **Revelstoke Railway Museum** was an interesting stop for train buffs. From there we went on to **Three Valley Gap**, just outside Revelstoke where we stopped for lunch. It's a great little "ghost town" with lots to see. Cost $12. We booked lunch in advance to save time (call 250 837-2109). Best to call if you plan to stop there as it's a very busy place as lots of bus tours stop there. We got a great hot lunch for $18 Cdn., including coffee and dessert.
There's another little vintage auto museum just down the road from Three Valley. It's on the right-hand side of the highway heading west, but the turn comes up fast around a corner with lots of traffic. It's called **White Auto Museum** and cost $6 for the museum, but the really cool antique shop filled with car stuff is free and all the 100s of autos on their lot are for sale. Best to call ahead as the place is perpetually for sale so you never know for sure if they'll be there. 250 835-2224.

At Kamloops, we stayed at the Hampton Inn, 1245 Rogers Way, phone 250 571-7897. Some of our cars were leaving the tour the next day, so we had a pizza party that night (ordered and delivered from Papa John's Pizza just down the road.) Cost worked out to about $6 per person. The hotel, very generously, let us use their breakfast room, which was big enough to hold all of us.

DAY 7. After bidding farewell to some of our friends, we continued on with 11 cars, heading for the coast. It was a lovely drive through B.C.'s Cariboo country. From Kamloops, we took Hwy 5 towards Merrit, turned off on Hwy 97C towards Logan Lake/Aschcroft. This road is off the beaten path and not so crowded. Lovely scenery. You'll pass the massive **Highland Valley Copper mine** – there's a viewpoint. Please stop and wonder at the scourge mining makes on the landscape. But don't beat up us Canadians over it – you probably have copper wiring in your vehicle.

Once we got to Aschcroft, we followed Hwy 1 to Lytton and then north on Hwy 12 to Lillooet (pronounced lil-oh-wet) where we stopped for lunch. Then, not wanting to go down the Fraser Canyon and struggle through the big city traffic of Vancouver, we set out on Hwy 99 (Duffy Lake Road) to Pemberton and Whistler. This is quite a scenic windy highway with few places to stop and take pictures of the pristine mountain lakes in this area but worth the drive.

At Whistler, we checked into the Aava Whistler Hotel, recommended by the BC Corvette club. Price was $216 for one night and $153 for the second night as it was a long holiday weekend. The rooms were small with very tiny bathrooms. No breakfast included, but there was a good breakfast at the Crystal Hotel across the street. Having been used by the Corvette club before, the hotel was great about cordoning off a section of their underground parking for us.

The next photo was taken at Whistler Peek, where the Gondola starts. From left to right, Tom and Carrole Helman, Dianne Johnman, Lana and Dan Rodlie and Roger Johnman.

DAY 8 – We spent two nights at Whistler and enjoyed the shopping, the nightlife, the **Peak-2-Peak Gondola** ride and all the hubbub that Whistler has to offer.

DAY 9 – It was down from the mountains on the Sea to Sky Highway. We stopped at the award-winning **Britannia Mine Museum**, which was a great place to learn about B.C.'s mining history. (Rated 4.5 by Trip Advisor). Cost $30. We booked ahead for a group tour (mandatory if you want the underground mine tour) and I think we got it for about $25. We timed our travel to be there for the 10 o'clock tour (about one-and-a-half hours from Whistler). From there, it is only a half hour to the ferry terminal at Horseshoe Bay. Absolutely make a reservation if going to Vancouver Island at a cost of $17 plus the ferry ride ($68), as you don't want to be waiting all day for a ferry, especially if you are traveling on a weekend. We arrived in Nanaimo around dinner time and booked into probably the best hotel of the tour thus far: Inn on Long Lake, 4700 North Island Highway. It doesn't have a restaurant, but there is a mall and other places to eat nearby. This place was lovely, with decks off the rooms that looked out over a lovely little lake. www.innonlonglake.com Cost was $161 Cdn, including breakfast.

DAY 10 – We took the highway down to Victoria following the old highway most of the way, stopping briefly at **Chemainus**, a town that has become world-famous for its murals. Since we arrived early in the day, there was lots of parking along the highway at the edge of town. Folks parked and walked the few blocks to see the murals.

From there we pulled onto the Island Highway towards Victoria at Duncan, our next stop **Butchart Gardens** for lunch and spent the rest of the day touring the gardens. This is a must-see if going to the island – absolutely breath-taking florals no matter what time of year. Expect to pay about $32 although they have different rates for different times of the year, plus special rates for groups. We found it expensive to eat or drink there, but then what do you expect for a touristy place?

From Butchart we drove the backroads (not recommended without a guide) through the residential areas of Victoria along the ocean. Some really beautiful places along there, but easy to get lost.

We then booked into the Harbour Towers Hotel, which I won't go into because it has since closed. (Too bad as it was a terrific place.) We went for dinner at the Blue Crab – touted as the best seafood place in Victoria. Don't believe it. There are plenty of great seafood places in Victoria. The Blue Crab is much over-rated.

DAY 11 – This was an open day when everyone went on their own to do whatever they wanted. Some folks from the Victoria Corvette club met us for lunch and offered to help with tours. The Royal B.C. Museum is worth a trip, but there is also whale-watching, the Parliament buildings, harbour tours and much more. I highly recommend you go on a red-bus tour (leave the car at the hotel). There are plenty of hotels downtown where you can leave your vehicle and just walk around. We stayed two nights.

DAY 13 – Some folks departed for Anacortis to head back home through Washington State, but the rest of us took the ferry from Sydney (Swartz Bay) to Tsawwassen (pronounced Ta-<u>wah</u>-sen). From Tsawwassen, you can easily take the highway towards Hope, B.C. This highway is so new, it was not picked up on the GPS so don't try to follow your technology. Just follow the signs. While we drove all the way to our home to Trail, B.C. (about 400 miles), some of the Americans stayed in Osoyoos (pronounced Oh-<u>sue</u>-yus) at Lake View Motel and Suites (250 495-7641). This has been a great retreat for car show people as the motel is really nice, large rooms with two or three bedrooms for big families or sharing couples. It's also off the beaten path so is away from the tourist places along the main drag. Nice BBQ area and pool. From there, it's about four or five hours to Spokane (I think).

DAY 14 – Those who hadn't left already, headed home with (we hope) a much better understanding of what we have up here in Alberta and British Columbia.

Forgot to mention the gift exchange thing – we've done this on every caravan.

While out and about, looking at the sights, trolling through museum gift shops or just buying gas, we play this little game. Everyone must buy a gift ($5 maximum) for a gift exchange. Don't tell anyone what you got. At some point along the trip, we stop and do an exchange that goes something like this: all gifts are put in a pile and everyone who bought a gift takes a gift – either from the pile, or from someone else who has already taken a gift from the pile. Of course, you can't open said gift until everybody has one. It's fun. We did our exchange in Kamloops before some of the "caravanners" left. Someone went home with a tiny jug of maple syrup from me, and I am now the new owner of a mood ring.

If anyone is planning this trip, or any part of it, and wants more complete directions, email me for the actual directions, maps, and highway numbers, or anything else you need to know.
Safe travels.   lana_rodlie@telus.net

Kelly Ham 2nd - Hayden, ID
The Saga of his 1972 Corvette Coupe

I ran into a friend that said he had a 1972 Corvette he kept stored in a barn and needed to sell it because he had fallen into hard times.   He told me it was a 1972 numbers matching car that needed a lot of TLC and a person with my patience and exceptional care to detail and finish putting it together.

When I learned the numbers matched I thought what a rare find it could be. We came to an agreement on a very fair price for this car. I inspected the numbers and sure enough they did match. We tried starting the motor, after it had been sitting for 12 years and it didn't go well.   It ran very rough and had a very odd "metal" noise so we shut it off and I thought I better tear it down and do a further inspection.

We found that it had flattened one of the lobes on the cam at #1 cylinder.   Maybe from a possible bad previous break-in. We found out the engine had a rare set of heads off a 1967 427, 435hp Vette.   Under advisement of another good friend, Roy Langlitz, we took the motor to Mike Rice, owner of Performance Associate Speed and Machine Shop at 6711 E. Seltice Way in Post Falls, Idaho.   Mike said it should be a great engine after he "baked" and had it "bead" blasted.   The motor had already been bored out to 60 over and with those heads and a set of rare pistons and the right cam as well as a nice 850 Holly carb, Mike felt it would make an awesome motor for the Vette.

This is me, Kelly 2nd, with the beard, Mike from Performance and my Dad, Kelly Sr.

At the time there were a lot of people wanting those heads, but we went ahead and had Mike build one of the nicest motors I had ever heard or seen.   Mike is a perfectionist and it showed in this motor. He builds some of the best race engines in the country.   I can't say enough thanks to Mike for building this awesome power plant - with over 500 horse power.

We are taking our time with the rest of the car trying to take care to details.   With the help of my daughter Aurora, and a few years, the car will be painted the original "Steel City Gray".   It should be a "keeper", and maybe someday Aurora will enjoy it.

END

NOTE   My thanks to all the wonderful folks who contributed these great stories and awesome photos. I hope you have enjoyed this book and either own a Corvette of your own, or will be inspired to get one.

I would also like to thank my wonderful Jerry for all the time he spent proof reading for me and for his patience and understanding while I had my nose in this book, gathering the material during the last year and putting it all together.   We both love our Corvette and have enjoyed sharing our story and learning about so many other, really great people. My thanks also to Gary Lee for his help in getting the book to the publisher.

NOTES

56885691R00058

Made in the USA
Columbia, SC
03 May 2019